Archbishop Daniel E. Pilarczyk

THE PARISH: WHERE GOD'S PEOPLE LIVE

PAULIST PRESS
New York and Mahwah, N.J.

Cover Photo: The Crosiers/Gene Plaisted.

Library of Congress Cataloging-in-Publication Data

Pilarczyk, Daniel E.
    The parish : where God's people live / Daniel E. Pilarczyk.
        p.   cm.
    ISBN 0-8091-3299-0
    1. Parishes—United States. 2. Pastoral theology—Catholic
Church. 3. Catholic Church—United States.   I. Title.
BX1753.P5   1992
250—dc20   91-42032
                                                    CIP

Published by Paulist Press
997 Macarthur Boulevard
Mahwah, New Jersey 07430

Printed and bound in the
United States of America

CONTENTS

INTRODUCTION

Most Catholics know what parish they belong to. In some of the larger cities of the Archdiocese of Cincinnati, people introduce themselves by their parish. "Hello, Archbishop. I'm Pete Schwartz. St. Antoninus." In some of the smaller places in our archdiocese, the parish and the town are the same, so that when people say where they are from, they are also telling you their parish. We have St. Rose parish in the village of St. Rose, and St. Wendelin's in St. Wendelin.

Catholics know what parish they belong to because the parish is important to them. Ultimately this importance arises from the fact that it is through the parish that we relate to the church and identify ourselves as church members. The parish is both the basic delivery system of the church's ministry, and the local community in which we are called to make our personal contribution to the church's life—a contribution not just of money but of time and energy and love and concern as well.

Everybody lives in a parish: active and inactive Catholics, atheists and agnostics, Protestants and Jews. Everybody lives in a parish simply because everybody—or almost everybody—lives somewhere, and because almost every "somewhere" in the world is included in a parish. That local congregation bears some responsibility, not just for those persons who come to church with regularity, but for everybody who lives within its territory. Everybody lives in a parish, and most Catholics know which parish is theirs. Yet our system of parishes is not as simple as it seems at first glance. For one thing, although most Catholics rightly look on the parish as their connection with the church, the basic unit of Catholic life is not really the parish.

When theologians and canon lawyers speak of "the local church," they don't mean parish but diocese. The diocese is the local church because it is the diocese which guarantees the fullness of church life. Through the local bishop the diocese offers officially certified church teaching. Through the local bishop, priests and deacons are ordained for the service of the people of God. Catholics are in union with the church universal through the union of their bishop—and therefore of their diocese—with other bishops throughout the world, the chief of whom is the pope, the vicar of Christ. On a more pragmatic level, most parishes are simply not able to provide for themselves the full range of resources that they need—books and programs for liturgy or catechetics, for example, or academic resources for the training of religion teachers and other lay ministers. This has to come from the diocese.

At the beginning of the church's life, there were no parishes. In its youthful days, the church was primarily an urban phenomenon. Christian believers lived in cities and in each city there was one Christian community, headed by the local bishop. The bishop was helped in his ministry by priests who formed a kind of committee of assistants and advisors for him. When the Christian faith spread to rural areas, the bishop would send out priests to celebrate the eucharist for the country folk on Sunday, but the basic community remained the city congregation under the leadership of the bishop. As these rural communities grew, the priest no longer went out just on Sunday, but took up his residence in the country, and so parishes were born. Eventually, as the number of believers grew in the cities, subsidiary communities were established there, too, and so the church had city parishes as well as country ones.

This historical development resulted in a kind of ongoing tension between parish and diocese which continues today. This tension manifests itself in the natural inclination of Catholics—laity and priests—to look out for the needs of their parish first and to think of the needs of the diocese second, while the bishop must look first to the well-being of the whole local church, even if this means that he must make demands on the parishes which are not always appreciated by everybody in the parish. Thus there is in Catholicism an essential universalist element—the diocesan element that keeps us catholic—as well as a more local element that gives us something smaller and more immediate with which to identify.

But this local, territorial, aspect of the parish has itself undergone development in the last few decades. In the past, Catholics belonged to the parish in which their home was located and that's all there was to it. (There might be exceptions for ethnic groups, whose parish was determined by whether they were German or Irish or Italian, but even in those circumstances, parish was a given.) Now, however, the territorial nature of the parish is less rigidly observed. Because of a local rule here in the Archdiocese of Cincinnati, for example, Catholics can belong to any parish they wish, provided only that the pastor of the parish to which they want to belong, if it is different from the parish in which they reside, is willing to accept their membership.

There are positive and negative aspects to this arrangement. On the positive side, people are able to worship and serve in whatever parish community they find themselves most at home. If they find themselves out of sympathy with the priest who is assigned to the parish in which they live, they are free to look elsewhere. On the negative side, this arrangement enables people to determine their primary point of contact with the church, i.e., their parish, on the basis of elements such as the quality of music or the availability of Catholic schooling. These elements are really secondary. Such an approach to parish may lead people to conclude that we need not make any particular effort to get along with a given mix of people if we do not find them particularly attractive, that we are free to pick and choose those with whom we will worship and serve the Lord. In an extreme form, the ability to choose one's parish could result in a whole congregation of people whose attitudes and tastes are the same, a congregation which would not welcome persons of different mentality, and which would therefore give a false or deficient witness to the all-embracing catholicity of the church.

For the vast majority of Catholics, however, the parish is the territorial parish in which they live, a parish composed of all kinds of people, a parish which forms an important part of their local community, a parish which has its own life but which at the same time is a unit of the real local church, the diocese.

In this book I wish to reflect with you about parish: what it means, who ministers within it, how its people are involved in it. I will have something to say about the various aspects of its life and activity, and about the challenges which it faces.

It is not my intent to provide an exhaustive theology of parish, nor to treat of all of the provisions of church law which relate to parishes, but rather to reflect with you as bishop of a local church on certain aspects of this highly important part of the church's community life.

As I begin, there are two points that I wish to emphasize. The first is that the vigor of the life of the local church, the diocese, depends very heavily—I am tempted to say *almost exclusively*—on the vigor of the life of its parishes. The diocese is more than a collection of parishes, to be sure, yet it is almost impossible for me to imagine a diocese in which the church is alive and well, but in which the parishes are weak and ineffective. Perhaps an analogy would be a physical body which claimed to be healthy, but in which the heart and lungs and brain were functioning poorly. The body as a whole can't be in good shape unless its major parts are also healthy. Consequently, when people ask me what the priorities of our local church are, I respond that the most important thing from my perspective as bishop is to have good parishes, parishes which are able to provide their members with a varied and vigorous church life, parishes which are concerned with more than survival.

Secondly, I wish to emphasize that parish life is a many-sided and variegated thing. It means different things to different people. Parishes vary from place to place in size, in tone, in emphasis. But one thing is common to every parish: complexity. A parish is not just a vehicle for running a school or a catechism program.

I have subtitled this book "Where God's People Live" to emphasize this complexity. Living implies variety and change. It implies tension and fulfillment. It implies receiving and giving. It implies relationships. All this is part of the life of individual human beings. All this is part of the life of God's people as a whole. For most of us, the context of our life as members of God's people is the parish.

My intent in this book is not only to reflect on the elements that make up the parish but also to convey some sense of—and gratitude for—what it means for God's people to be alive there.

Questions for Reflection

1. What parish do I belong to? Why?

2. What do I know about the life of my parish, about what goes on there?

3. What does my parish do for me? What do I do for it?

WHAT IS A PARISH FOR?

Before we can discuss the details of parish life, we have to be clear about the purpose of the parish. Basically, a parish is a community of men and women united in the Lord in order to be God's people. A parish is the church in miniature, and so whatever is true of the church at large is true, in some degree at least, of the parish.

First of all, therefore, parish is a gift because the church is a gift. Neither the church universal, nor therefore its smaller components, is something that we make for ourselves personally, but rather something that we receive from God as a sign and agency of God's love for us.

This love is not something that we deserve or earn. It is a gift, given just because and only because God has chosen to love us. There is no compelling reason why God should pay any attention to us at all. After all, we are tiny creatures, living on a pinpoint in the cosmos. God created us simply because He decided it was a good idea. God stood by us even when our first parents turned from him. God came to be one of us in Christ Jesus and still lives in our midst, not because God owes us anything, not because we deserve God's attention, but just because, for some inexplicable reason, God loves us.

In addition to that, God chose to involve human beings in expressing his love for us. The life that he continues to live in those who believe in him is not just an interior relationship between God and the individual, but a love affair that extends to all of us through each of us. We are all called to be agents of God's care and love to each other. This is not an individualistic endeavor, but rather something that we are called to carry out in collaboration with one another. Each of us is a continuation of the life of Christ, and all of us together form one body of Christ. The body of Christ, this ongoing presence of God in our midst, is the church and the local, grass roots expression of the church is the parish.

A parish, then, is a moment, a chapter in God's love affair with us human beings, and being a member of a parish does not mean just "belonging to something" but rather being involved in a loving association with God in Christ Jesus and with each other in him, and with all the world for him.

Parish is therefore concerned with relationships—our relationship with Christ and our relationship with each other in him. Consequently, the main participant in every parish is the Lord himself. It is he around whom the people gather in worship. It is he whose word the parishioners hear there. It is his work that the parishioners carry out in the context of the parish's life and in their activity in the world, activity for which they are enlightened and strengthened in the parish. It is for the strengthening and expression of his body, the church, that the parishioners build buildings and carry out programs. It is in response to his love that the parish engages in care for the poor and in outreach to those who have forgotten Christ or have never known him.

Our relationship with God involves both receiving and giving. So does our relationship to the parish. In the parish we receive God's gifts. Most of us were incorporated into the life of Christ in baptism in the parish of our parents. We are drawn together and strengthened in that life through the parish eucharistic celebration. Our sins are forgiven in the sacrament of reconciliation there. Marriages are blessed, the sick are anointed and the dead are given their final commendation in and through this agency of God's love for us. Through the parish we are instructed in the word of God from infancy through adulthood. God touches our lives through the kindness and affection of our fellow parishioners. We do not and cannot deserve any of this. It is all ultimately the freely given gift of a loving God who keeps in touch with us through this specific portion of his church. The parish is where we receive much, perhaps most, of what God wants to give us through his church.

Because of this, we are also called to give in the parish. God's love for us demands to be shared with others, with those specific others with whom we are associated in the local community. There are lots of ways in which we share God's love in parish life. We encourage one another in our faithfulness to worship just by being there together on Sunday morning. We help parents educate their children through our support for the parish school and religious education programs. Through our prayers and our concern for the sick of the parish we extend the love of Christ to them. Even in the parish's social activities we are expressing the love of Christ for the people around us, the love of the Christ who so enjoyed the company of his friends.

This is why the territorial nature of the ordinary parish is important. Every parish contains a more or less random mix of women and men, gathered into one local community because they happen to live near one another. It is to these persons that God invites us to extend his love. We don't choose those to whom we wish to relate in Christ. They are given to us by the Lord in the community to which we happen to belong—attractive people and boring people, people we like and people we are not particularly fond of, people we are well acquainted with and people we may not even know. All of them have a particular claim on us just because we form together this small portion of the people of God.

The common element of every parish, then, is God's gift of himself to us in Christ, a gift of love which invites us to receive and to give in turn to others, a gift that is offered to everybody. A parish may be big or small, rich or poor, urban or suburban or rural. But, no matter what its circumstances, every parish exists in order to manifest and share the generosity of God. That's what a parish is for, because that's what the church is for.

All this suggests several things to be careful about in our relationship with our parish and our attitude toward it. For one thing, a parish is much more than buildings. Appropriate buildings in good repair are important because people need to have a place to meet in order to carry out the activities they wish to engage in: worship, schooling, socializing, or whatever. But buildings are not and must never be an end in themselves. If we are not clear about their connection with the life of the Lord Jesus, they can be a burden rather than a blessing.

The same thing is true of the programs and activities that the parish engages in. The parish does not exist just in order to keep the priest and the people busy. In fact, if the programs and activities do not have their focus in the life and love of Christ, they are useless, if not downright harmful.

We also have to be careful about our attitudes toward the priest and people who make up the parish. We'll be saying more about this later, but from the very beginning it is important for us to acknowledge that Christ does not live only in perfect people or talented people or pleasant people. Christ lives in all of us, and if we are too critical of our priests or our fellow parishioners, if we hold back in our participation in the parish's life because we think that people like these aren't really worth our time and effort, we may be depriving ourselves of important gifts that Christ has in store for us through them.

Finally, we have to beware of looking on the parish as a kind of convenience store or service station which we take advantage of when we want something but which is of no particular concern to us at other times. Every pastor laments the parishioners who offer nothing to the parish to make its life more vibrant, but who appear out of nowhere, it seems, to demand special services and special attention when they have need for them. It is not that these people haven't "paid their dues," but rather that they seem to think that the parish is some sort of social service agency rather than a community of believers which exists in order to share the love of Christ.

The parish, then, is more than buildings and programs. It is not an exclusive association of virtuous and committed people, but an ingathering of all sorts of men and women. The parish is the church in miniature, a community of ordinary people beloved by God and striving to respond to that love in their faithfulness to God and in their dedication to one another. In the last analysis, the answer to the question, "What's a parish for?" is that a parish's purpose is to enable people to be Christian believers. A parish is for Christ.

Questions for Reflection

1. What would my life be like without my parish?

2. In what ways do I see Christ in the priests and people of my parish?

3. What connection do I see between the activities of my parish and Christ's love for me?

THE PRIEST

Every parishioner in every parish is called to represent Christ to the other parishioners and to the world at large. Every parishioner is an agent of Christ's love.

The parish priest is called to represent Christ in a special way. He is to be the agent of Christ, the head of the church, a representative of Christ, the leader of his people.

In the immigrant church of a few generations ago the leadership role of the priest was clear and obvious to everybody. He was generally the best educated person in the community. He had answers to every question. He was the one church-person who looked after everybody and everything. His word was law and his authority unquestioned.

Things are somewhat different now. Catholics generally are better educated, and so the priest is not the only one with answers. As a result of a higher degree of sophistication among the people, they no longer respond so readily to "orders" from on high. Moreover, life has become more complex and people have greater expectations from their parishes. They need more highly organized programs of preparation for the sacraments for themselves and their children. They want to be involved in programs of social action and service to the poor. Religious education is no longer a matter of teaching catechism answers to children—if, indeed, it ever was—but a lifelong process that reaches from pre-school years throughout adulthood. Youth groups have been part of parish life for some time. But now, in addition to that, there are senior citizens' groups, support groups for the divorced, prayer groups, and day care centers. The priest is no longer able to do it all personally. Instead of being the one agent of the church in the community, the priest is now one minister among many.

Yet the parish priest is still the leader of the parish. He represents the headship of Christ in the parish in a way in which other members of the parish and other representatives of the parish do not. He is the parish's good shepherd, its pastor.

In speaking of the priest as the representative of the headship of Christ in the parish, it is important to recall that Christ looked upon his own leadership role as a role of self-giving and of service. "The Son of man came not to be served but to serve and to give his life as a ransom for many" (Mark 10, 45). He spoke of himself as the shepherd who lays down his life for his flock (John 10, 11).

This means that the priest is not "the boss" who has the right to order his subordinates around in any way he wishes and to have his own will carried out just because he wants it that way. He does not represent himself but the loving and caring Lord Jesus.

But if the priest is not "the boss," pure and simple, neither is he an employee of the parishioners. Just as they are not there to do his personal will, he is not there to carry out their every wish at the risk of being harassed, ignored, or fired. There is a deep spiritual significance to the fact that the priest is *assigned* to the parish by the bishop. He is not hired or chosen by the people. He is sent there by the bishop, who represents the leadership of Christ in the local diocesan church. He is sent to this particular unit of the local church to represent Christ's leadership there. There is a certain "givenness" about the parish priest, just as there is a certain "givenness" about the diocesan bishop and a "givenness" about Christ and about Christ's love for his people.

There are several details of the priest's service as pastor which make the nature of his leadership role more clear. First of all, the parish is not "his." It is Christ's parish and the church's parish, and he is there to represent Christ and the church. Hence, the pastor is not free to do as he wishes with the parish to which he is assigned. He is bound, of course, by the general law of the church and by local diocesan regulations. But more than that, his work as pastor is to be shaped by the demands of Christ's love for his people. The pastor is not a free agent, but a representative of the Good Shepherd.

This is one reason why parish priests in many dioceses are transferred to other parishes with some regularity. No priest, no matter how holy or how talented he may be, can totally and adequately represent the fullness of Christ's concern for his people. Some priests are better preachers than others. Some have a greater sensitivity in ministering to the sick or the bereaved. Some are more deeply interested in education. Some have organizational and administrative skills that others lack. But, humanly speaking, no one priest can be everything for his people or do everything for his people that Christ desires. Hence, the present practice of moving priests around is a reminder to pastor and people alike that the priest is a representative of Someone else and that that Someone is never fully or adequately represented by any human agent.

According to the law of the church, the pastor is responsible for the governance of the parish, subject to the ultimate authority of the bishop. He is the one who hires and retains parish employees and who must account for the spiritual and material condition of the parish. No action of the parish council or of other parish advisory bodies has any canonical effect without the consent of the pastor. This is not a legal provision established to resolve power struggles, but another way of saying that the priest's ministry does not come from the people but from Christ.

Moreover, there can be no parish which does not have the pastoral care of a priest. Even in remote areas where priests can come only rarely, and where someone else has been put in charge of tending to the day-to-day life of the congregation, the church's law calls for a priest to be the official, canonical pastor. The reason for this is not to keep control of the church in the hands of the clergy, but to indicate that there is a need in every area of the church's life for the kind of Christ-like leadership that can only be expressed by the priest pastor.

The priest, then, is the leader of the parish who represents the servant headship of Christ. Whatever his talents or deficiencies may be, whatever his skills, whatever his rough edges, whether the parishioners find it easy or difficult to deal with him, he nonetheless brings to his people the love and the care of Christ, the Good Shepherd.

This places great responsibility on the priest. He is not free to do what he wants and then take refuge behind the authority of Christ. He is there to serve, to love, to care for, to teach the people of the parish. He is there to lead them in worship, to extend to them the compassion of Christ in time of trial. The servant leadership of Christ is present even in the least effective pastor, but all pastors have the responsibility of reflecting as fully and as adequately as they are able the One whom they represent.

Most priests find the peak point of their priesthood in the celebration of the eucharist. This is understandable if we remember that it is in presiding at the eucharist that the priest most clearly represents the servant leadership of Christ. Gathered in the midst of his parishioners, the priest preaches in the name of Christ and then, as their representative and his, joins in Christ's giving of his life and his work to the Father. As representative of the people, the priest expresses their gift of themselves. As representative of Christ, he expresses Christ's gift of himself for them.

Perhaps it is also worth pointing out that parish priests are called to, and in fact do, love the people they are sent to serve and to lead. Often it is difficult for a pastor to find ways to tell his people how much they mean to him, especially if there are several thousand of them. Occasionally limitations of personality on the part of the priest or of some of the parishioners seem to give more prominence to misunderstanding and conflict than to affection. But the fact remains that priests give their lives to the leadership service of their people. No consideration is supposed to have greater weight in the life of the priest than the well-being of his people. This is not to say that the parish priest doesn't need some time off for rest and care for himself, but even this is only to enable him to serve them more generously and more effectively. If love means wanting good and doing good for the beloved, then every parish priest is engaged in a full-time love affair with his parishioners.

It's not a bad way to spend one's life.

Questions for Reflection

1. What differences do I see in the ministry of my parish priest from the way it was when I was a child?

2. What qualities do I see in my parish priest that reflect Christ's concern for me?

3. Have I ever offered affirmation and encouragement to the priests who serve me in the parish?

MINISTRIES

"**M**inistry" used to be a Protestant word. There were Baptist ministers, but Catholic priests. When someone went away to study for ministry, it meant that they were going to be in charge of a congregation that had Bible study at nine o'clock and a Sunday worship service at ten-thirty.

Now "ministry" and "ministers" have become Catholic words, too. We have extraordinary ministers of the holy eucharist and programs for training in lay pastoral ministry. Even priests now talk about their priestly ministry, whereas in the past they talked about their apostolate.

What's going on here? What does "ministry" really mean?

The word "ministry" means service. Any service that somebody does for somebody else can be called ministry. But there is a narrower meaning of the word that has become current in the last decade or so. In this narrower sense, ministry is a service that is performed in the context of church. Because this usage of the word is relatively new, at least among Catholics, its exact limits are still not clear.

There are some who would confine "ministry" to those services performed in the name of the church by one of its ordained ministers. Thus, one could speak of the ministry of priest or deacon, but not of the ministry of the lay director of religious education. As a kind of appendage to this use of "ministry" are the ministries of reader and acolyte. These

17

ministries are officially conferred by the bishop on persons who will exercise some permanent service in reading God's word or in assisting at the altar during the eucharist. In practice, the formal ministries of reader and acolyte are usually conferred only on those preparing for ordination to diaconate or priesthood.

Others would extend the use of "ministry" to include everything that a Christian believer does in the service of his or her neighbor. Thus, a visit to a sick friend could be called ministry, as could the practice of comforting people in their times of sorrow and disappointment.

The question of how to use the word "ministry" in some consistent fashion is presently under study by church authorities and scholars. The purpose of the study is to clarify the term, so that we all mean the same thing when we use the same word.

I am inclined to think that "ministry" is best reserved for some activity done in the name of the church by a Christian believer with the authorization of some church authority. Thus, the minister would always be to some degree an official representative of the church, accountable to church authority for what he or she does. If the term is used in this way, the second grade CCD teacher would be an official minister of the church because his or her activity is done at the request of the parish director of religious education, ultimately under the authority of the pastor, and would represent the parish in the context of the second grade CCD classroom. On the other hand, a mother of a second grader who teaches her children, and perhaps some neighbor children, about Jesus and the church is performing a service of charity which may have the same effect as the work of the official CCD teacher, but it is not ministry because it is not done under the official auspices of the parish.

I believe that this sort of distinction between "official" ministry and the "unofficial" activity of Christian believers is important, because it enables us to identify who is working in the name of the church and who is not, and also because it establishes clear lines of accountability. For one thing, the church cannot make itself officially responsible for everything its members do, no matter how generous and helpful those services might be. Moreover, if everything is ministry, then nothing is really ministry, and we would have to find a new term to describe the work done by representatives of the church in the name of the church. Conversely, not every act of Christian service requires official approval. Not everything has to be designated as ministry to have any worth.

The reason why "ministry" has become current in Catholic circles is that the church's service has expanded so wonderfully in the past few decades that its former sole ministers, priests and religious, can no longer do it all. This is due in part to declining numbers of priests and sisters, but it is also due to increased opportunities for service as Christian life has grown more complex, and to the increased capabilities of lay women and men to provide official service. There is more to be done than there used to be, and there are more people who are able to help do it.

Not too long ago the position of director or coordinator of parish religious education was a new thing, and people wondered exactly what these persons were supposed to do. Today, many parishes have somebody exercising this function. The same is true of youth ministers, parish visitors of the sick, coordinators of programs for the divorced and remarried, directors and collaborators in the RCIA, business managers, and special ministers of the eucharist. Most parishes have had organists and ushers and secretaries for quite a while, but now we see that they, too, as official agents of the church's work, also share in the church's ministry.

There are three further comments that need to be made as we consider nonordained ministry in the life of our parishes. The first is that we should not see lay ministry in our parishes as a temporary expedient that will disappear when we once more have as many priests as we used to have. There is no reason why priests and religious have to do everything. And there is likewise no reason why the baptismal gifts and natural talents of lay people should not be put at the official service of the church. I believe that most pastors would agree that parish life has been deeply enriched by the work of lay ministers, and that our parishes would be deeply wounded if they were suddenly to disappear. Apart from any other considerations, the presence of lay ministers in a parish can enable the priest to give greater attention to those tasks which are particularly his: overall leadership, preaching, and the celebration of the sacraments of reconciliation and eucharist. The priest's image as representative of the headship of Christ is much clearer if the priest doesn't also have to be bookkeeper, liturgical reader, and day-to-day director of the parish school.

But to say that lay ministry is a gift to the church is not to say that everything that can be done by a lay person should be done by any lay person at all, whether qualified or not. Twenty years or so ago, folk music groups were the rage. It was thought that all the parish needed was a few young people who knew how to play the guitar and sing, and the youth of the parish would flock to Sunday liturgy. This theory has been proven untrue, and part of the reason is that so many of the folk music groups just weren't very good at what they were there to do. Then there are liturgical readers. It is no service to the church to have lay readers do the first two readings at Sunday mass if they are so unskilled that nobody can make sense of what's being read. (I myself often wonder about the wisdom of having a terrified youngster do the readings at confirmation. The congregation, far from being able to pay attention to the word of God, generally sits on the edge of the pew to see whether the reader is going to survive the experience.) Good will is a great thing, but it cannot take the place of talent, training, and practice. Just as the priest must train for his role in the church, so also lay ministers require training and practice, in addition to natural gifts. The length and complexity of their training depends on the degree of responsibility they are preparing to assume.

Lay ministry, then, is not a temporary expedient for a passing moment in the church's life. Nor is it a task that is to be taken on without adequate preparation. It is a gift to the church that must be received with reverence, both by the minister and by those the minister serves.

Finally, lay ministry is not the be-all and the end-all of the lay state. It is simply untrue to suggest that a lay person's life is only of value to the extent that he or she dedicates his or her talents to the direct, authorized service of the church community. Lay people, precisely by reason of their vocation as lay people, are called to represent Christ in the world: in their families, their neighborhoods, their work places, their civic communities. The church exists to strengthen and prepare them for these responsibilities beyond the limits of the visible parish community. If we allow ourselves to become so fascinated with lay ministry within the church that we forget what the church's mission is, we do a disservice to lay ministers, to the church, and to the world.

Questions for Reflection

1. What activities in my parish are under the responsibility of lay persons?

2. What activities, programs, and services are there in my parish that were not there ten years ago?

3. How are people trained for lay ministry in my diocese?

PARISH COUNCILS

The parish is a community of believers striving to live out their life in Christ together, in need of strength and inspiration to carry him out into the greater world in which they live. Their leader is their parish priest who represents the servant leadership of Christ in the midst of this group of people. He is assisted in his responsibilities by other ministers who work in the name of the parish under the pastor's direction.

One might conclude from this that the task of the pastor is simply to tell his people what Christ expects from them in the parish and in the world and then send them away to do it. After all, he is their leader. But it's not that simple.

For one thing, the lives that the parishioners lead are increasingly complicated and demanding. Not everybody's circumstances are the same at home, at work, or in the civic community. For another, there is a wide variety of possibilities in the services that the parish can provide. Granted, everybody needs the sacrament of reconciliation. Everybody needs to take part in the celebration of the eucharist. And, of course, everybody should contribute to the financial needs of the parish! But beyond those basics, there are choices to be made. Is the parish ready for a renewal program? How can the church's task of evangelization be carried out in this particular area of the diocese? Is it time to beef up the religious education program for high school students? What kind of support and direction do these particular people need in their daily lives? Would an opportunity for some formal scripture study be welcome, or a prayer group? What about a chance for parishioners to discuss the challenges they find in their business and professional lives? Are there problems like alcoholism and spouse abuse that need to be addressed by the parish leadership? If so, what are the best ways to address them?

All of this suggests that the members of the parish have to have a voice in the life of the parish if the parish is going to be for them what they have a right to expect it to be. The pastor and his coworkers are not all-knowing. They are not mind readers. If their ministry is going to be effective, they have to listen to the people they are there to serve.

Much listening can take place informally. After all, the pastor and the parish ministers do not live and work in a world apart. They know the people they minister to, many, perhaps most of them, by name. They know the general circumstances of their lives. They are in daily contact.

But sometimes informal listening is not enough. Sometimes it is necessary to have structured mechanisms for listening to insure that the listening really takes place, and that what needs to be said does get said.

The structured mechanism for listening that has developed in our parishes since Vatican II is the parish council. In its most effective form which, to be sure, is not found everywhere, the parish council is a representative group of the entire parish organized in such a way that all the voices of the parish can be heard and somehow responded to. Likewise, in its most effective form, the parish council is the means by which the pastor and his associates in ministry can test their own ideas and proposals with a group that reflects the whole parish community. The parish council, then, is a gathering of the whole parish, through its representatives, for the purpose of dialoguing with the parish's leadership about the life and activity of the parish. It is an agency of planning and evaluating, a place for the sharing of wisdom and reflection. It is the official listening post for the local parish community—the pastor listening to his people and the people listening to their pastor.

The parish council and its more specific offshoots, such as the parish education commission or finance commission, are not legislative bodies in the sense of having the right to make rules which the pastor and the rest of the parish are compelled to follow. They are consultative groups. Sometimes it is said that they are "merely" consultative, but I find that the additional adverb is misleading. It could give the idea that, because they are "merely" consultative, they are therefore of no importance. It is true that the final decisions are the pastor's and that the parish council and its subsidiary groups have no binding authority apart from him. But if those decisions are going to be the best decisions, the pastor has to know what is going on in the parish. He has to know what the people expect. He has to be aware of what they are capable of. He has to consult. If he does not, he runs the risk of leading the parish in a way which is irrelevant to its members, or in a direction in which the parish will not or cannot follow. A good pastor never thinks in terms of his parish council as "merely" anything, because he knows that his pastoral ministry is hampered and undermined without it. The parish council is not just one more thing the pastor has to contend with. It is one of his most important links with the reality of those he is sent to serve.

If the parish council is to do what it is supposed to do in a parish, several things are necessary—in addition to faith, prayer, and attentiveness to the Spirit on the part of all who are involved in it.

First of all, it has to be set up in such a way that the people of the parish are adequately represented. Sometimes a parish council is composed only of the heads of various parish organizations or programs. This is appropriate as far as it goes, but, structured in that way, there is no representation of the ordinary members of the parish who, for whatever reason, are not able to give their time to special projects and activities. It is important that there be representation of the parishioners at large.

Then the parish council and the pastor have to be clear about what their purpose is. If the members think that their role is to dictate the direction of the parish, or if the pastor thinks that this is just one more group of people he has to meet with before he goes off and does what he intended to do in the beginning, there is going to be trouble.

Thirdly, the parish council and the pastor have to know each other well enough to engage in a relationship of trust, to risk sharing their needs and their views with each other. This implies a certain frequency of contact. If the parish council does not meet regularly, or is kept only for emergencies, its effectiveness will be very limited.

Pastor and parish council members have to treat each other with respect. They cannot afford to engage in manipulative tactics. They cannot allow any of the council's members to monopolize the meetings or use the council to further his or her own special interests, even if those interests have a certain importance. They are there, all of them, priests, religious, lay persons, to serve the common good of the whole parish. Sometimes interpersonal tensions will occur which will need to be dealt with, either by encouraging people to work the tensions out among themselves, or by taking advantage of the services of a facilitator or an expert in group dynamics. The council is too important a part of the parish's life to allow itself to be paralyzed by the antisocial behavior of any of its members.

Sometimes differences of opinion will arise between different groups on the council or between the pastor and the council as a whole. In these situations the pastor certainly has the right to say, "Look, I am the pastor and this is what we are going to do." But generally it is better to try to come to some sort of agreement that everybody is at least partially satisfied with. This may mean postponing a decision until a future time. It may mean consulting the parishioners as a whole through some sort of questionnaire. It may be good for each group or party to try to express what they think the others are saying, so that at least the various positions are clear. In any case, it is almost always counterproductive when a decision is made which results in some being winners and others perceiving themselves as having lost.

Parish councils are characteristic of a maturing church. They are not always effortless. Sometimes they can be very painful for parishioners and pastors alike. But when they work well, they are highly encouraging signs that the life of Christ is active in all the components of the parish and that the voice of the Lord is being heard.

Questions for Reflection

1. How does the parish council function in my parish?

2. Have I ever been a member of parish council? Would I be willing to be a member if asked? Would I volunteer?

3. What is my connection, as an individual parishioner, with my parish council?

EVANGELIZATION

We have spoken about what a parish is and what it is for. We have said something about the pastor and his coworkers and about the structures which provide its members with a voice in its life. Now it is time to say something about the specific activities of the parish.

I have chosen to begin with evangelization because evangelization constitutes the basic agenda item that underlies everything else the parish is supposed to be concerned with.

"Evangelization" means sharing the good news which formed the kernel of Christ's mission on earth. That good news is that God loves us human creatures in spite of our sinfulness and narrowness and selfishness. It is the good news that we don't have to, and, in fact, that we cannot, earn God's good will and care, but that God is passionately concerned about us just because we are his creatures. It is the good news that our lives have meaning and purpose because of God's interest in us. It is the good news that none of us is insignificant in God's sight. It is the good news that God has plans for us to be happy in his company forever. It is the good news that what God asks of us is simply to accept his love and let him live in our lives through the continued presence and activity of Christ in us.

Many Catholics look on evangelization as something new in the church, a new "program" of things to do that somehow came out of the Second Vatican Council. This is a correct perception, in one way, yet an inexact one. One of the basic thrusts of Vatican II was to bring the church back to basics, to help its members realize that being a member of the church is not only a matter of holding certain beliefs and engaging in certain practices, but of opening ourselves up to God's love and carrying out the consequences of that love. Evangelization, i.e., hearing and passing on the good news that Christ offers us, is a "new" concept in the church only insofar as we had tended to overlook it in the past, perhaps because we were too intent on some of the secondary features of the church's life. In these last few decades the church has been saying to us, "Let's not forget what we are really all about." What we are really all about is evangelization.

The call to hear and respond to Christ's good news is a call that every person needs to hear. Those who are already active members of the church need to be evangelized because they, we all, run the risk of zeroing in on short-term concerns and forgetting about the reason why we are members of God's people to begin with. Even parish leaders can become so involved with parish council and special collections and leaky roofs that they lose sight of the fact that all those matters, important as they are, must somehow be directed toward accepting and responding to God's love for us. If we don't hear the good news regularly, we may end up forgetting who we are.

Those who are less active members of the church, the women and men who are not particularly prominent in the life of the local church community or who only take part in the parish's life occasionally, or whose faith is superficial, need to be evangelized in order to become more aware of God's concern for them, of the gifts that God has given them and continues to give them, gifts that they may overlook or underestimate as they busy themselves with the nitty-gritty elements of their day-to-day life.

Those who are not members of the church community

at all need to be evangelized, too. They need to hear that there is more to their lives than making a living, that God has in mind for each one of them a purpose and a destiny that reaches far beyond their petty successes and satisfactions, far beyond their problems and puzzlements. They need to be reassured that each of them is personally important and personally loved by a personal God in the person of Jesus, and that they are personally called to be a member of God's people.

How does the church go about carrying out this responsibility to proclaim the good news that Christ came to offer to us? Everything the church does is supposed to have an evangelizing dimension. Everything that happens in the parish, is supposed, in some way, to proclaim God's love and invite our response to that love. This is the purpose of the preaching and teaching that takes place in the context of the parish. This is what our liturgical worship is intended to express. This is why parishes have youth programs and sports teams and bereavement committees and support groups for the divorced. In some way or other, it is all intended to call us to an awareness of God's love and to remind us of the response to that love that God expects of us.

Occasionally, perhaps at budget planning time, parishes conduct a review of their activities and programs. It seems to me that when such a review is done, we have to keep asking ourselves how each component of the parish's life contributes to its mission of evangelization. Whatever does not contribute in some fashion to the proclamation of God's love for us, whatever does not enable the parishioners to respond more effectively to that love is at best irrelevant and at worst counterproductive.

In these last few years the church has given us a new instrument of evangelization. This is the Rite of Christian Initiation of Adults (RCIA). The RCIA provides direction for parishes in receiving new members. It is not so much a program that the parish engages in from time to time as an ongoing process that is supposed to be a constant part of the parish's life. It is not an optional activity for parishes which wish to use it, but is intended to be an essential element in the life of every parish, an element as essential as liturgy and education.

The RCIA is primarily directed toward those who have never been baptized, but it has also proved helpful in the reception into the church of those who have previously been members of other Christian communions and in bringing back inactive Catholics to the full practice of their faith.

One of the most appealing features of the RCIA, in my judgment, is that it involves the whole parish. The priest and the catechists and the sponsors are most closely involved with the prospective new parishioners, but from time to time during Lent those who are to be received into the church on Holy Saturday are presented to the parish at large. The purpose of these presentations is to ask for prayers for the candidates as they walk their journey of faith, but it is also to remind the parishioners at large of the gift that they themselves have received and to make them aware of their responsibility to invite others to share in the blessings of faith. The RCIA is an instrument of evangelization for new members of the church, but it is also an instrument of evangelization for those who are already parishioners, as well as a call to them to become evangelizers themselves. The RCIA teaches all of us that life in Christ is a gift, a gift that we are called to acknowledge and to share.

Evangelization, then, is not so much an activity as a mind-set and an attitude of the heart. In parishes where evangelization holds its rightful place, the parishioners see their faith, not as a burden or a source of obligations, but as a gift, as *the fundamental* gift that God has given them, as the gift that gives sense and meaning to everything else in their lives. Parishioners who are aware of the meaning of the good news of Christ are eager to reach out in love to their fellow parishioners, to engage in worship with gratitude and enthusiasm, to share their resources of talent and time and money in response to God's generosity to them. Parishioners who are aware of the good news of Christ are anxious to let other people know the source of their life's meaning, not necessarily by ringing doorbells or handing out pamphlets on street corners (although these things can sometimes be part of particularly intense evangelizing efforts), but by letting themselves be seen as women and men of hope and fulfillment who are willing to talk about what their faith means to them. When the author of the First Letter of Peter said, "Reverence the Lord Christ in your hearts and always have your answer ready for people who ask you the reason for the hope that you all have" (3:15), he was speaking to us—about evangelization.

We are called—all of us in every parish—to be the community of those who bear witness to and proclaim the good news of Christ. Unless we are able to do that, unless we are willing to do that, we are not really being what Christ meant his followers to be.

Questions for Reflection

1. How is my parish an evangelizing community?

2. Do I need to hear the good news of Christ? Why? When?

3. In what way am I an evangelizer?

LITURGY

If evangelization constitutes the bones and muscles of the parish, the essential framework on which everything else depends, the liturgy is the community's heart and voice.

Liturgy is the parish's heart because it is in liturgy that the people as community open themselves up to God's word, to the renewed proclamation of God's interest in and concern for them, to the special expressions of God's love for them which are the sacraments. Liturgy is a particularly intense moment in the love relationship between God's people and its Lord. It is an affair of the heart.

Liturgy is the parish's voice because when the parish gathers for worship it proclaims its identity before God: this portion of the pilgrim people, beloved by God, gifted by him, responding to his love in praise and thanksgiving, aware of its own continued need for God's attention.

But liturgy is more than a gathering of parish members. Liturgy also involves Christ. In the church's official corporate worship, Christ is present and active. He praises and prays with us. He speaks to God in our name. With the parishioners, Christ stands again before the Father to offer his love and our love, his sacrifice of himself and our sacrifice of ourselves. In the liturgy Christ strengthens us and inspires us to continue our life and our activity in him in every aspect of our human existence.

This is why Vatican II called the liturgy the source and

the goal of Christian life. (*Constitution on Liturgy*, 10) It is the focal point to which we bring our efforts and needs, and from which we take away the reassurance and strength of Christ.

There are many forms of liturgical worship in the church's life: funerals and weddings, baptism and confirmation, celebrations of the sacrament of anointing of the sick. All of these are expressions of the heart and voice of the parish. All of these are contact points between God and the community of believers. But the most usual forms of liturgical worship are the sacrament of reconciliation and the celebration of the eucharist. These are what most Catholics refer to when they speak of "receiving the sacraments."

Many people do not look on confession, the sacrament of reconciliation, as a celebration, but as a duty. We do, in fact, have an obligation to confess our serious sins and ask for God's forgiveness for them. We need to acknowledge in a personal and explicit way our sinfulness. If we don't, we run the risk of forgetting who and what we are. But that's only a part of the sacrament of reconciliation. The more important part is the proclamation of our forgiveness by Christ through the ministry of the priest. In the sacramental absolution we hear Christ saying to us, individually and personally, that we are loved in spite of our sinfulness, that he loves us so much that he can never forget about us; that our lives are too important to God ever to be written off as a bad investment. In the sacrament of reconciliation we also hear Christ saying to us that, although our sins have harmed the community of the church, we are still members in good standing as long as we are willing to acknowledge our need for his forgiveness. The sacrament of reconciliation, therefore, is more than our having to admit that we have been bad. It is a sacrament of freedom and healing, a celebration of God's love for us and of God's mercy toward us as individuals and as members of his community.

Many parishes find that these celebratory aspects of the sacrament of reconciliation are best highlighted in communal celebrations of the sacrament during Advent and Lent, when the people gather together to hear God's word, to examine their lives, to acknowledge their sinfulness, and to receive individual absolution in the context of their local parish community. It is hard to look on confession as a grim duty when it takes place in the joyful presence of Christ in the midst of his people.

The most frequent expression of liturgical worship in the parish is the celebration of the eucharist. In the mass we have the clearest manifestation of the voice and the heart of God's people united with Christ.

There are many forms of eucharistic celebration ranging from the quiet weekday celebrations through the crowded splendor of midnight mass at Christmas. The "standard" celebration is the Sunday eucharist when the parishioners come together in larger numbers for the official expression of their Christian identity as parish. But every eucharist is a sharing in Christ's offering of himself in sacrifice to his Father in association with his faithful people.

Every eucharist is an effective re-presentation of Christ's offering of himself. The mass doesn't depend for its basic results on the holiness of the priest or the people, or on the quality of the reading and the music. Christ is there for us, no matter what.

Yet, if the eucharist is to be most beneficial for those who participate in it, more is required than just saying the words and doing the actions. Good liturgy takes preparation and care. The priest has to prepare his homily thoughtfully, so that the word of God comes to his people in ways that they can best understand and assimilate. The music has to be a source of inspiration rather than of distraction, and so it must be good music. The way the readings are done, the attitudes of the ushers, the expertise of the ministers at the altar, even the way the collection is taken up—all these make a contribution to the atmosphere in which the heart and the voice of the parish are raised to God. Good liturgy doesn't just happen.

But it is not just the priest and the other leaders of the liturgy who have a part to play. Every member of the congregation has a contribution to make to the corporate worship of the parish. The basic contribution that each parishioner is expected to make to the Sunday liturgy is to be present for it. Sometimes people underestimate the effect of their absence on this fundamental expression of parish life. In addition to that, though, all the parishioners are called to be actively engaged in what is going on, to respond to the prayers, to take part in the singing, to share in and extend the sign of peace. Going to mass is not a private affair. It is participation in a corporate celebration, and it is no more appropriate to wish to be "left alone" at mass than it is to go to a party and sit solitary in a corner.

Sometimes people complain that they don't get anything out of going to mass on Sunday. In many cases, this is because they come to mass with the wrong expectations. The Sunday eucharist is not an entertainment. We are not there to be amused or to be delivered from boredom. We are there to give—to give the support of our presence to our fellow parishioners, to unite our prayers and our praise to that of the other members of the parish, to express our need for Christ's word and Christ's presence in our lives. If it is true that each one of us has our part to play in the celebration of the eucharist, then it is simply unfair to come with the expectation of being part of the audience. There is not supposed to be an audience at mass, but only participants.

Occasionally people find going to mass on Sunday to be unsatisfying because the liturgy just isn't all it should be or could be. In such cases, the parishioners have the responsibility of working with their pastor to improve the quality of the liturgy—the music, the physical surroundings, the reading of the scripture, the quality of preaching—so that the Sunday mass is the kind of occasion that the church means it to be.

But the fact remains that every eucharistic celebration is a call for the giving of ourselves with Christ to the Father, and if we approach it only with the idea of getting, we are sure to be disappointed.

Most parishes give a high priority to the quality of their liturgy. Liturgy commissions, under the leadership of the pastor, see to the allocation of appropriate resources for the liturgy. They prepare carefully for reconciliation services and for the celebrations of the eucharist. They search for ways to improve their fellow parishioners' understanding of the liturgy and their participation in it. And this is as it should be, because good liturgy, well prepared and joyously shared, is an impetus toward and a reflection of everything else that goes on in the parish. If the heart and the voice of a parish are not strong, neither is the parish.

Questions for Reflection

1. What do I expect when I participate in the liturgical life of my parish?

2. What do I contribute to the liturgy?

3. Why do people stay away from mass on Sunday?

EDUCATION

Parishes have bones and muscles: their awareness and acceptance of the good news of Christ. In the liturgy parishes have a heart and a voice. Parishes also have a mind that needs to be enriched and informed if the parishioners are to respond appropriately to God's good news of love and to participate fruitfully in the parish's worship. This is why every parish is an educational institution.

Before we talk about the educational endeavors of the parish, it might be useful to specify what we mean by education. Education is more than schooling. If we identify education with going to school, we are limiting it to a very narrow range and we run the risk of thinking that once we have graduated from school—whether it be high school or an institution of higher learning—our education is over.

Education is also more than acquiring information. To be sure, a significant part of education means learning facts and the relationship of the facts to each other. But that's only a precondition for real education. Real education has to do with personal development, with growth in our appreciation and understanding of the way things are and of why they are that way. A deeply educated person is not just one who knows things, but one who is a mature, articulate, compassionate, generous human being whose way of living is shaped and transformed by what has been learned.

If education is more than schooling and if it has to do with the life and development of our human personhood, it follows that our education is never complete as long as we are still alive. We might turn that statement around and say that once we decide that our education is over, we have really stopped living. In our earthly existence, at least, education and development and life all go together.

This is true of human life in general and it is also true of our life in Christ. We always need education in our faith because our faith is always in a state of development. This is why every parish is concerned with education.

Parishes carry out their educational responsibilities in many ways. Liturgy is one of the more important educational instruments of the parish. In the liturgy we hear the word of God in scripture proclaimed and explained. We deepen our personal development by our participation in the community's worship. In praying together, in offering our praise and thanksgiving as a parish community, we come to a greater awareness of who and what we are, both individually and corporately. As we celebrate the important points of human existence in the liturgy—birth, maturity, marriage, sickness, death—and as we recall our sinfulness in the sacrament of reconciliation and our need for unity and nourishment from Christ in the eucharist, we learn about ourselves and about God. But if the educational component of the liturgy is to have its effect in us, we have to pay attention. We have to make the effort to understand not only what God is doing in the liturgy, but also what God is teaching to the community at large and to us as individuals.

Most of the parish's social programs have an educational component as well. The youth group does not exist only to provide young people with something to do, but also to teach them about themselves and about each other. A senior citizen's club provides the opportunity for older persons to share their experiences with each other and so to learn from each other. Many pastors have found that even annual parish festivals, in addition to bringing an economic benefit to the parish, are also an effective educational experience, an experience which teaches about dedication and self-sacrifice, about collaboration and, sometimes, about patience and forgiveness. But in all of these contexts, just as in the liturgy, we have to pay attention if personal development is to take place. We cannot be educated against our will, and if we refuse to look for the deeper significance of what we do in our parish community, we will be limiting ourselves to superficial busyness.

Then there are the more clearly educational activities of the parish: scripture study groups, lecture series, workshops and the like. Every parish has, or should have, a certain number of such opportunities, not only because of their inherent worth, but also as a reminder to the parishioners that their education is not yet finished.

The most obvious educational activities of most parishes are concerned with children and young people, and with good reason. These members of the parish are still at the beginning of their personal growth and are still acquiring the basic education in faith that will serve as a foundation for the rest of their lives. This is why parishes are called to provide the best possible education in faith to *all* the children of the parish.

There has been some controversy about the quality of Catholic religious education both in and outside of schools. In the past, it seemed that learning about one's faith consisted of memorizing catechism answers. Then, for a while, it seemed to some that academic content had been totally sacrificed to "feeling good about Jesus." Today we are probably reaching a bit more of a balance. Publishers of religion textbooks are very careful to provide sound Catholic doctrine in their books. In most dioceses, those who teach religion are expected to have a certain level of professional training. And there has been a growing realization that religious education has to strike a balance between content and commitment, between head and heart. I believe that most pastors and parents and bishops are happy with these latest developments. Certainly they are all grateful to the women and men who dedicate their energies to the religious education of the church's young people.

There has been controversy about Catholic schools, too. Twenty years or so ago many people were saying that parishes with a Catholic school allotted a disproportionate amount of their resources to a small percentage of the parishioners, and that the church might be better off if Catholic students all went to the public school. Today sentiment seems to have shifted. Careful studies have shown not only that Catholic schools provide a general education that is better than that provided by most public schools, but also that adults who have been educated in Catholic schools tend to be in closer touch with the church than those who were not.

Several things seem clear. One is that the secret of the academic success of Catholic schools lies in the familial support that lies behind them. Every student in a Catholic school is there because somebody (generally parents) decided that the student should be there and because somebody is willing to make the sacrifices necessary to keep the student there. Another thing that is clear is that a daily program of religious education, for 180 days a year, in a deliberately Christian school community, provides a kind and a degree of religious education that no other kind of program can provide. A third thing that is clear is that Catholic schools are expensive. There is the tuition cost to the parents, but this only covers a portion of the actual cost for educating each student. The remainder must be taken care of by the parish. Some parishes find that almost all their resources go to maintaining the school, and that everything else, including religious education programs for children not in the school, are suffering. When this happens, it is probably time for the parish to begin looking toward a consolidation with another Catholic school so that costs can be reduced. Church leaders around the country are continuing to try to find new ways to provide some sort of financial relief that will enable us to offer Catholic schooling to the maximum number of students. A fourth thing that is clear is that a large proportion of parents want good Catholic schools for their children. There is no more predictable source of turmoil in a parish than the suspicion that the school is going to close or that it needs improvement.

Parishes are concerned with the education of their parishioners because education is part of life. Some of the parish's educational undertakings, like the school and the religious education program, call for support from every sector of the parish. Others may be of interest only to a few parishioners. But no parishioner, certainly no parish, can afford to overlook or play down education, because education is essential for the growth and development of our life in Christ.

Questions for Reflection

1. How does my parish offer education to its members?

2. Do I look to my parish for education? Why? Why not?

3. How well informed am I about the church and its teachings?

STEWARDSHIP

Sometimes people claim that all they hear about in church on Sunday is money, and that the only thing their pastor seems to be interested in is increasing the collection.

When I hear people say things like this I wonder if they have really been paying attention. I am tempted to ask people who complain about how often the priest preaches about money to keep an honest and accurate count for a year and see whether their perception has any accurate foundation, or whether it merely reflects their own unwillingness to hear about money at all. (I would not include in the challenge the notices in the parish bulletin which detail how much was received last Sunday as opposed to how much is needed each week, because such notices are probably extensions of an accountability program which the pastor and his advisors have devised to keep the parishioners informed about how things stand.)

I don't know any priest who enjoys talking about money. Most pastors speak about parish financial needs once or twice a year, and then only because they have to. Sometimes the parish finance committee has to harry the pastor in order to get him to do that much. Most pastors are really embarrassed to talk about money. They would much rather talk about the scripture readings for the Sunday, about God's love for his people, about Christian moral life.

Why, then, is money an issue at all in Catholic parish life?

There are several reasons. One is that money is the primary material resource of the parish community. Granted, the love of Christ is not bought by money, nor do the sacraments depend for their effect on any offering made by the recipients. But beyond those fundamentals, almost everything else that happens in the parish depends to some extent on how much money is available. There will be no church building to worship in unless there is money to build one. There will be no light and heat unless somebody helps pay the bills. There will not even be a eucharist unless somebody can provide enough money for the pastor to buy some bread and wine.

Moreover, there are always further needs to be met. No matter how great the parish's income may be, there are always more things to do, more forms of ministry which would benefit somebody in the parish community, more claims outside the parish on its generosity. It is practically impossible for an active parish with a sensitive pastor to have too much money—or even enough!—simply because money is a precondition for ministry and because there are no limits to the ministry that the church can and should provide.

In addition to that, many Catholics seem to expect to be served by the church for nothing, or for almost nothing. Let it be clear that no parish may confine its attention to those who contribute at a certain level. The good news of God and his sacramental outreach to his people are not for sale. But the fact remains that in most parishes about 70 percent of the parish income comes from 30 percent of the members. Many parishioners seem to make the same dollar contribution that they did ten or twenty years ago, as if rising costs do not affect religion. Others express their differences of opinion with the pastor or the diocese through the medium of the collection basket. Others just don't seem to care about the needs of their local Christian community, yet they expect it to be there when they need a priest or when it is time to send their children to school.

These are just a few of the reasons why pastors have to deal with money, even though they don't like to. They certainly don't want to harp on the subject. They certainly don't like to suggest that some of the parishioners they love are really freeloaders. When pastors talk about money, it is almost always because they are convinced that they have to, not because they want to.

Over the last decade or so a new approach has arisen for dealing with the resource needs of the parish. It is called stewardship. It is an approach that has been common to other faith communities for some time, but which is new to Catholic congregations.

The basic idea of stewardship is that people should not contribute to their church merely in response to its needs, but rather in proportion to what they themselves have received from God. What we give to our local church community should not be just enough to pay its bills, but enough to be an adequate expression of our gratitude to God for God's generosity to us.

The word "stewardship" suggests looking on what we have, not as our own possession, but rather as something entrusted to us by God. A steward is a trusted collaborator of the master, to whom the master's resources have been committed, not for the well-being of the steward, but for the purposes of the master. A good steward is one who makes use of what has been entrusted to him (or her) to further the master's wishes. An unworthy steward is one who forgets that the resources are not personal property but a trust, and who begins to act as if he (or she) were their outright owner.

God has entrusted all kinds of gifts to us. God gives us the gift of time—a series of ongoing opportunities to do things for him. God gives us our talents—that unique mix of capabilities that enables each of us to make our own personal imprint on creation. And God gives us money. We tend to think of money as particularly our own, as something we have earned and which is therefore ours in a special way. Yet, if we reflect a bit, it is easy to see that our economic wealth is a result of gifts and opportunities that are beyond our own accomplishment. None of us is self-made. Whatever we are and whatever we have are the result of "accidents" of birth, of personality, of chances that we have had for no apparent reason. And yet, our faith teaches us that all this is not really a matter of "accident" at all, but of action on our behalf by a loving God. Nothing is really ours. It is all entrusted to us by God for his purposes. We are stewards, not owners, and we have to remain conscious of our status as stewards.

This doesn't mean that we have to impoverish ourselves in order to acknowledge our indebtedness to God. After all, one of God's purposes in entrusting these gifts to us is so that we can enjoy them and make use of them for our own development in the context of his love. But we have to take care to remind ourselves that what we have is only a loan, a loan not just for our benefit but also for the benefit of others whom God loves as God loves us.

We remind ourselves of our dependence on God and we express our role as God's stewards by deliberately sharing our time, our talent, and our financial resources with others as agents of God's love for them. This sharing need not be confined exclusively to sharing with our parish, but some of the sharing should be directed there, because it is there that we explicitly experience and express God's love and concern for us.

Those who are convinced of their stewardship responsibilities, therefore, will look for ways to give time to the needs of the parish. They will look for opportunities to make their talents available for the service of the parish. And they will share their financial resources with the parish, too.

Sometimes people wonder what kind of financial assistance they owe to their parish. A good rule of thumb is tithing, the giving of one tenth of our gross income to charitable purposes, including, of course, our parish. Experts in stewardship suggest that a good steward will give five percent of his or her income to general charitable causes—United Appeal, diocesan needs, and charities that one is personally interested in—and five percent to the parish. Sometimes it takes a little planning and a little cutting back on other expenditures to reach this level of giving, but we can be sure that the effort we make to express our dependence on God and our gratitude for what God has given us will not put us in the poorhouse. In fact, most people find that their generosity to their parish and to other charitable causes results in further blessings from God, broader and deeper than what they have given.

Being a member of a parish means being part of the family of God, a family which is cared for in numberless exquisite ways by its Father. But being a member of a family doesn't mean just receiving. It means responding, too. And one of the ways we respond to our Father's love is through responsible stewardship of his gifts.

Questions for Reflection

1. When did I last hear the priest preach about money at Sunday mass?

2. To what extent do I share my time and talent and financial resources with my parish and with other worthy causes?

3. What gifts has God given to me?

DIFFICULT PEOPLE

Every parish has some difficult people in it, and they come in all shapes and sizes.

There are the people who criticize everything. No matter what is done, no matter what happens, it is always wrong. There are not enough flowers on the altar, or the pastor is spending too much money for flowers. The school is using up too great a part of the parish resources, or the parish isn't doing enough to provide Catholic education for its children. The bishop isn't paying enough attention to our congregation, or the bishop should leave us alone. These are the persons who seem to need to assert their own individuality by tearing others down.

There are also the people who aren't very good at what they do, but who can't be removed to make way for others: the reader that nobody can understand, the usher who carries on loud conversations with his friends during the Sunday liturgy, the CCD teacher who can't teach, the bingo worker who doesn't show up most of the time. Some members of the parish think that these people should simply be told that they aren't needed any more. Others, generally including the pastor, think that the harm done by the deficiencies of these people is more tolerable than the hurt that would be inflicted by telling them that their gifts, limited as they are, aren't wanted by the parish.

There are the single-issue people: the parish council member who never wants to talk about anything but finance;

49

the head of the athletic boosters who seems to think that the parish exists for the sole purpose of sponsoring basketball teams.

Sometimes the difficult people are those who seem to find it impossible to forgive or forget a hurt that they received from the parish in the past. "Father chewed out the best man at my daughter's wedding." "The principal expelled my grandson from school." "The organist refused to play my mother's favorite hymn at her funeral." Often these injuries were not inflicted last week or even last month, but five or ten years ago. The people who suffered them just don't seem willing—or able—to let them go.

Sometimes there are people in the parish with personal disorders of various kinds who feel a compulsion to call the rectory every day or so, or who take every possible occasion to latch onto other parishioners and tell them their troubles.

Every parish also has a significant group of difficult people who are takers, those who do not participate actively in the life of the parish, who don't contribute in any significant way, but who nonetheless expect that the parish and all its resources will be there for them whenever they need them. These may be the persons who are most difficult of all for the pastor as he struggles to keep things going and is then informed by men and women he has never seen before that, no matter how much he has done for the parish at large, he hasn't done enough for *them*.

Sometimes it is the pastor himself who is a difficult person in the parish. Every priest's gifts and energies are limited. No priest can possibly do everything that everybody expects of him. When a new pastor comes to a parish, there is always a comparison with the previous pastor. Often this comparison is unfavorable to the new man, just because people have not yet had a chance to learn what new strengths and insights he has to offer the congregation. Sometimes a priest is sent to a parish precisely because it is clear to the bishop that some changes need to be made there, and these changes are not popular. Occasionally a kind of communal personality conflict arises when it seems that this particular priest just can't get along with this particular community. And sometimes the priest becomes a difficult person for the parish because he makes honest mistakes in his leadership of the parish: mistakes of judgment, mistakes of sensitivity, mistakes of tone.

What is a parish to do about its difficult people? One approach would be to get rid of them one way or another. In this approach, the difficult people would be given to understand that they really don't fit in here. They would be invited to stop doing the things that annoy other people, to try harder to fit in, to keep quiet, or else to get out of the way and go somewhere else. At the very least, they would be given to understand that the parish really doesn't want to spend time and energy dealing with people like them.

Another approach would be to tolerate the difficult people, to reach the conclusion that there isn't much that can be done about them and that therefore they should be treated with benevolent indifference. "Don't pay any attention to her. She has been around the parish for years and Father doesn't know how to get rid of her. You have to take the bad with the good around here."

A more Christian approach is to love the difficult people. If Jesus expects us to love our enemies, he certainly expects us to do the same for the people whom we merely find difficult. This is not to say that people should be encouraged to do whatever they want in the parish, no matter how much their behavior harms or annoys others. Difficult people do have to be dealt with, but they have to be dealt with in the awareness of Christ's love for his people, rather than in an effort to have a tensionless parish in which everybody agrees about everything, and everybody is just like everybody else.

It may be that difficult people are among God's gifts to us because they serve to keep us conscious of several important truths for our Christian existence.

One is that Christ did not call us to a church in which everything has reached a state of ultimate perfection. In his parables of the kingdom, Jesus speaks of weeds and wheat, of good fish and useless fish, of wise virgins and foolish virgins. It seems that he found it necessary over and over again to insist with his disciples that the community he came to found is not yet complete, and that in their zeal to throw out everything that they thought didn't fit, they ran the risk of doing away with much that would ultimately prove serviceable to God. The church and its parishes are always a bit messy, a bit ragged, a bit uneven. Catholicism is not a religious faith that demands perfection as a condition for membership, but rather one which offers hope and acceptance to everybody who is willing to try to respond to Christ's love. To reject the difficult people is to try to make the church into something that Christ never meant it to be. Our responsibility is to love our brothers and sisters in spite of their deficiencies, in spite of what they may have done to us. It is not our responsibility to judge or to reject.

Another truth that difficult people teach us is that we ourselves don't have all the answers, either. Sometimes in what the difficult people say or do there may be a lesson that we need to learn. It may be the lesson of compassion and forgiveness. It may be a new insight that the difficult person offers the community and that the community is unwilling to accept.

That brings us to the third truth that difficult people may have to teach us: at one time or another, in one way or another, we are all difficult people. None of us is without our rough corners or our limitations. The qualities that seem to us to be our virtues may very well seem like defects to somebody else. Achievements that we are proud of may be annoyances to other people in the parish. If we are unwilling to offer loving acceptance and patience and forgiveness and attention to people that we find difficult, we may be preparing a pretty cold reception for ourselves in a different time and in different circumstances.

Difficult people are important in a parish. They are signs of the Lord's universal love for his people. They remind us that God's grace and God's salvation are not extended just to people whom we happen to like. They keep us aware of some of the more demanding aspects of our faith. But most of all, the difficult people whom we try to work with, whom we try to understand, whom we try to love and forgive are a sign of hope for each one of us that there will be warm acceptance and affection for us when *we* are the difficult people.

Questions for Reflection

1. How do I react to the difficult people in my parish?

2. Why does Christ love those who cause such annoyance to others?

3. In what way am I a difficult person?

"OUTSIDERS"

In every parish there are difficult people. These are persons who account themselves members of the parish in good standing and who, in various ways, cause annoyance and discomfort to the other members of the parish. But in every parish there are also men and women who really belong to the church but who, for various reasons, do not count themselves as members. Sometimes people refer to them as "lapsed Catholics." Sometimes they call themselves "former Catholics." Whatever the terminology, they look on themselves as "outsiders."

These are persons who cannot in good conscience receive the eucharist and who are not ready to come to grips with their personal situations through the sacrament of reconciliation.

Such persons include those who have left a valid, sacramental first marriage, have been divorced and have entered an invalid second union. They know that they may not receive holy communion, and so they conclude that the church simply isn't interested in them any more. They look on themselves as "outsiders."

So do homosexual persons who do not accept the church's teaching about sexual continence and continue to engage in homosexual activity.

Occasionally women and men who dislike what the church teaches about contraception or racial justice will move away from the church because they think that their own personal beliefs exclude any kind of relationship with God's people. Others are convinced that some past sin has rendered them unworthy of being in the church.

There are still others, perhaps many more than we would like to believe, who have simply slipped away. They begin by becoming irregular in their participation in the sacraments, and soon find that years have gone by without any contact with the church. They have become "outsiders" by default.

Each individual situation is unique, but all the "outsiders" have come to the conclusion that the church doesn't want them any more, and that therefore they want nothing more to do with the church.

How should the parish relate to such persons? There are two principles at issue here, and each of them must be maintained. The first principle is that the church, and therefore the parish, is simply not free to say that something that is wrong is really right. It is wrong to live in a conjugal union with a man or woman who is not one's spouse. Likewise it is wrong to engage in homosexual activity, and even more wrong to present such behavior as an acceptable lifestyle. It is not right to pick and choose those teachings of the church which one accepts and to reject the rest. It is not right simply to absent oneself from the life of the Christian community. The local parish must not give the impression that sinful behavior really doesn't matter or that each member is free to set up his or her own version of the faith. The local parish must remain faithful to the church.

At the same time—and this is the second principle that must be maintained—the parish is not free to determine that people whose lives or whose beliefs or whose level of practice are not everything that they should be are unimportant and can therefore be written off. Still less is the parish free to treat them as if they were no longer members of the church.

The model that the parish community must follow is, once again, the model of Christ who welcomed sinners and loved them while encouraging them to repent and leave their sinful ways, who spent his life trying to entice people to enter a love affair with God. The only people that Jesus was impatient with were those who were convinced of their own righteousness, the people who thought they didn't need him. Even then, he held out the hope of conversion and mercy.

In practice, this means that the parish must be a warm and welcoming community not only for those who feel at home there, but also for those who see themselves as "outsiders." Nobody can simply be rejected. If people cannot receive the eucharist because of the life they have chosen for themselves, they should at least know that they are welcome to attend the Sunday liturgy and participate in a less complete fashion. Everybody should know that the forgiveness of Christ awaits them whenever they are ready to accept it. Everybody should be aware that the Lord never writes anybody off, and that his local church community strives to follow his example.

The teachings of the Second Vatican Council provide a model which may be useful here. One of the most tormented questions that the council fathers dealt with was the question of membership in the church and of salvation outside the church. Who belongs? Do those who do not formally and explicitly belong still have access to the saving grace of Christ? The council resolved these questions by teaching that the saving love of Christ is present whenever people do what they can to respond to God's call in their lives and that, to the extent that they respond to God's love, they are members of God's people. Membership in the church, then, admits of degrees. The full members are those who, in the spirit of Christ, accept the church's teaching and sacraments and visible structure. (Cf. *Constitution on the Church*, 14) Others are members partially, to a certain degree.

It may be that this same sort of idea is true of participation in parish life on the part of church members. Some persons are able to participate fully, a participation expressed by their reception of the eucharist at the community's liturgical celebration. Others are limited by the situations in which they have placed themselves and so can participate in the parish life only in an incomplete way. Just as there are degrees of membership in the church, so there are degrees of participation in the parish.

It's not a question of not belonging, of not being a member. It's not a matter of really being outside the church, but rather of belonging and being active only to a certain degree.

But understanding the relationship of the "outsider" to the parish is not enough. If the parish is to be an adequate expression of the love of Christ, it must also approach the "outsiders" to invite and enable them to become insiders once more.

In order to be faithful to this responsibility, many parishes provide special programs for inactive Catholics. These programs offer dialogue sessions in which people are welcome to express their difficulties with themselves and with the church. The priest and those who assist him offer information about the church's marriage laws and about the means that are available to rectify irregular unions. They explain the church's teaching on all the points that people have problems with, and in the process offer opportunities to challenge and question. But above all, these programs strive to make clear to the participants that the church has not written them off, that Christ has not forgotten them, that no one is beyond the embrace of Christ's forgiveness, that there is no need for anybody to be an "outsider."

It is important for parishes—and parishioners—to remain conscious of their need to extend themselves to the "outsiders," because all of a parish's members, to a greater or less extent, for longer or shorter periods of time, have been or will be outsiders. Every time any of us sins, we distance ourselves from the Christian community. Whenever we are less than totally accepting of the church's teaching, whenever we refuse to play our full part in the life of God's people, whenever we are less generous than we should be to our brothers and sisters in the Lord—whenever any of that happens, we move toward "the outside." Most of us turn back before we get too far away, but the obvious "outsiders" are merely those who have continued farther in the direction in which each of us has walked at some time or another. If we refuse to extend the love and concern of Christ to them, we are implying that that same love and concern need not be extended to us.

According to the teaching and law of the church, once one has become a Catholic, it is simply impossible to stop being a member of the church. No matter what a person has done, no matter how impossible a situation a person may be in, no matter how long a person has been away, he or she still belongs. He or she still has a claim on the ministry of the church. He or she can still be forgiven. In the final analysis, it is impossible for any member of the church to become a true "outsider." And that is a truth that every parish is called to proclaim.

Questions for Reflection

1. Are their any "outsiders" among my family and friends?

2. What can I do to assure "outsiders" that Christ and the church still care for them?

3. To what extent have I ever been an "outsider" myself?

CLOSING PARISHES

It used to be a rare thing for parishes to go out of existence. Sometimes a government program of expressway building would come into an area and sweep away the parishes in its path. Sometimes a neighborhood would change to the extent that there were simply no people left there. But apart from situations like that, everybody always assumed that their parish would last forever.

That is no longer the case. Many dioceses are closing parishes these days, parishes that still have a Sunday congregation, parishes that are still ministered to by a priest. Some dioceses have closed dozens of parishes at one time. Some have closed them in smaller groups. Some have long-term planning programs to prepare congregations for the time when their particular parish may no longer exist.

What is happening? What does it mean?

The closing of parishes reflects new realities in the church and in society at large.

First of all, there is the diminishing number of priests. In some dioceses, one of the greatest problems that bishops faced in the past was finding ways to use all the priestly personnel that they had. Priests taught algebra and typing in high schools. All diocesan offices and services were directed by priests. Priests had to wait twenty years or more in order to have enough seniority to become pastors. New parishes were founded wherever the bishop thought there were enough people to support a priest. Now things are different.

Because we do not have as many priests as we used to have, they have to be more carefully apportioned. Parishes which do not demonstrate a certain level of Sunday mass attendance may find themselves without an associate pastor. Other parishes, with still smaller populations, find themselves sharing a pastor with a neighboring congregation. Still others are closed completely. Most dioceses simply don't have enough priests anymore to assign them as they used to.

The media would like to have us think that every time a parish is closed, it is because of the priest shortage. But, as is so often the case, the truth is more complex.

Parishes are also closed because they don't have enough people or enough resources. Expectations of parish ministry have changed over the last decades. In the past, it was enough if there was the regular celebration of the sacraments, if there was religious instruction for the children and, perhaps, a school. Today we have long periods of instruction before marriage and before the baptism of children. People expect that their parish will provide support groups of various kinds, prayer groups, scripture study groups. Preparing and carrying out the liturgy require much more effort than they used to. Organized evangelization efforts call for the participation of significant numbers of parishioners. Much more goes on in a parish than was the case previously. More collaboration is called for from more parishioners. If the parish is too small, if it doesn't have the means to provide what people need, it can sink into a kind of twilight existence in which it exhausts all its energy in just staying alive. In these situations, it is better to close the parish and bring the people and the resources it still has into a larger congregation. Everybody is better off.

There is also the question of expense. It costs money to run a parish, and the costs are not decreasing. We struggle to give better wages to priests and sisters and lay employees.

Many pastors find that aging facilities require large outlays of money. Is it better to spend all one's time raising money just to maintain buildings, or is it better to close and combine parishes so that financial resources can be more responsibly used?

Another factor in closing parishes is an everyday reality that we tend to take for granted: easy transportation. Many older parishes were established so that people could walk to church or so that they didn't have to go more than a mile or two with horse and buggy. This requirement is no longer an urgent one. People drive miles to get to work without complaint. They expect to have to use a car to get to the grocery store or the dry cleaner's. Even the people who don't or can't drive find that they can usually get transportation if they are willing to ask their neighbors to help them with a ride occasionally. We simply don't need parishes in every local community any more.

Closing parishes, therefore, is much more than a response to a priest shortage. It is also a strategy to help the church offer a stronger parish life to its members and to make more responsible use of the resources it has.

There is also the fact that parishes are never simply terminated and the people turned loose to fend for themselves. Parishes are generally merged with other parishes and the result is a renewed and more energetic congregation.

All this makes the closure of parishes more understandable, yet not necessarily easy. Bringing a parish community to closure is always painful: painful for its people, painful for its priest, and painful for its bishop. Every priest or bishop who has been involved in closing a parish has heard people say that their parents and grandparents were baptized there, that they themselves were married there, and that they had hoped to be buried from there. Parish closings bring sadness.

There is also a sense of failure, even of betrayal. For

decades priests and people gave of their time, their talents, and their money to support this local unit of the church. Working and worshipping together, they extended the life of Christ to each other. They cared for one another. They shared the love of Christ in their midst. They had a common experience of effort and struggle, of consolation and achievement. And now it seems to be all over. Everything they have done now seems to have been for nothing.

This sense of loss or failure is understandable, but it is not fully appropriate. A parish is a living community, and living things change. Parishes do not exist so that there can be buildings. They do not even exist so that this particular group of people can share common experiences. Parishes exist so that the life of Christ can flourish in the people of God. As circumstances change, the needs of God's people change. New arrangements are called for, new groupings, new approaches. If the life of the church is to be vigorous and strong, we simply cannot afford to hang onto all the old structures. Granted, we have grown accustomed to this group of people in this place. Granted, we take a rightful pride in what we have achieved in this particular parish. But all that is really secondary. What is primary is the preaching of the gospel, the appropriate celebration of the liturgy, and ministerial service that cares for the needs of all the people. When former arrangements make these things difficult or impossible, new arrangements have to be found. When the time comes to close a parish, the Lord asks us, "What do you really want? A living Christian community or a weak and struggling parish?" This is a painful question, but one to which there is only one correct answer.

There are other situations in our experience which parallel the closing of a parish. For example, the neighborhood "mom and pop" grocery store is no longer with us. It's not that people did not appreciate the convenience of walking down the street to buy a loaf of bread from people they knew, but that this small operation was no longer able to provide all the products and services that people wanted. Similarly, most of us remember our first car, how proud we were of it, how much we enjoyed the new convenience and independence it offered us. But almost nobody who is more than twenty-five years old still has his or her first car. The old car needed more and more attention, just to keep running. New models came along with new features. When it came time to get a new car, we discovered that we simply couldn't afford to hang on to the old one, no matter how fond of it we were. There was a certain sadness as we walked away from it for the last time, but we realized that life simply had to go on.

Sometimes it is hard to accept that life has to go on, but that's part of living. When parishes close, we are brought face-to-face with that reality in our common life as believers. God doesn't call us to live in a museum, no matter how familiar or how comfortable the museum may be. He calls us to live in his church, a church that is alive, a church that calls for new commitments and new efforts. Jesus said to his disciples, "Follow me." Following means that we can never stay put where we are. Following means the willingness to leave things behind.

Questions for Reflection

1. How many parishes have closed in my diocese in the last five years?

2. Are people generally better or worse off when their parish closes?

3. What does it take to keep a parish alive?

HOW ARE WE DOING?

The questions that arise about the closing of parishes raise other questions about the broader church. Are the new realities with which parishes are called to deal a sign of growth and vigor or of retrenchment and decline? If the parish is a unit of something larger—diocese and church universal—how are the bigger units doing?

There are a number of reasons for believing that the church has fallen on bad times. The number of priests and seminarians, at least in our country, continues to decline. Surely the apparent unwillingness of men to dedicate their lives to the service of the church is an indication that this service is no longer attractive, that something is wrong with the church that makes potential ministers back off.

Then there is the decline in mass attendance. Several decades ago about seventy percent of all available Catholics in our country attended mass every Sunday. Now the percentage is below fifty, in some places well below fifty.

There is also the apparent lack of knowledge of their faith that characterizes many Catholics. In times past, Catholics had learned answers to all the important questions through years of careful catechetical training. Now it seems rare for anybody under a certain age to possess even a minimum of ordinary Catholic knowledge.

Moreover, many Catholics simply refuse to be guided by the church. Every family has had the experience of some of its members falling away from the practice of their faith.

Statistics show that Catholics get divorced and have abortions at about the same rate as other people in our society. The church's teachings about contraception are often disputed and, it seems, disregarded. Catholics used to confess their sins frequently. Now, it seems, few go to confession as often as they used to, and more and more seem not to go at all.

Some people look on all of this as a sign that the church is in a period of serious decline. The reasons they offer for the decline are varied. Some say that it is due to the apparent unwillingness of the church's leadership to preach hell fire and damnation, to lay down the law for their people and let the chips fall where they may. Others say it is because the church insists on outmoded moral teachings, especially in the realm of sexuality. Some think that the Second Vatican Council changed the liturgy to such an extent that it is no longer the edifying mystical experience it once was, and now runs a poor second to the cartoons on TV. Others think that the church is in the state it's in because Vatican II didn't change things nearly enough, in the liturgy and elsewhere.

But, if indeed there is a weakening of the church, are all the reasons to be looked for from within? If people are apparently no longer as faithful to their religious commitments as they used to be, is the fault exclusively the church's? Is it significant that we are, by and large, the best fed, the best housed, and generally the most comfortable society the world has ever known? Is it significant that most Americans spend most of their free time watching TV? Is it significant that the sexual habits of our society are basically the habits of permissiveness whose only limits are a concern that we limit the transmittal of disease and try to see that "nobody gets hurt"? Is it significant that the achievements which our society prizes are basically non-Christian if not anti-Christian: success, security, painlessness, independence, self-fulfillment? These habits and these attitudes are the fabric of our culture. They are sold to us in every way that human ingenuity can devise. And they all have their effect on our religious attitudes. If there is a decline in religious observance, is it due to a failure of effort or creativity on the part of the church, or is it due to the tidal wave of the secularist culture in which we find ourselves engulfed?

But is there really a decline in faith? What about the numbers of lay women and men who choose to spend their lives in the service of the church as teachers in Catholic schools, as directors of religious education, as youth ministers, as parish business managers, as RCIA directors? Might it not be that the Catholic faithful today have more ministerial service available to them than ever before, despite the smaller number of priests? Is the church really worse off now that we have educated Catholics at every level of government, education, and business? Are Catholics in general worse off now that they can participate in a liturgy they can understand and assimilate? Catholics may be in closer touch with the word of God in the Bible today than they have been for centuries. Surely that is not a sign of decline. The openness of parishes to the contributions that parishioners can make in parish councils and parish commissions has enriched rather than impoverished the church. Is it not possible that, although numbers may be down, the quality of religious life may actually have improved?

These questions about the general state of the church are questions that all of us, including bishops, ask at some time or another. It is natural for us to want to know how things stand with something as important to us as the church. Is it improving or declining? Is it succeeding or failing? And why?

Yet these are questions to which we cannot give a definite answer, because some of the most important elements of the church's life are the elements that lie beyond our perception. We can count priests, and even predict how many there will be five or ten years from now. We can count how many people come to mass on Sunday, and make a pretty good estimate of how many should be coming. Every pastor knows how much money he needs to keep the parish going and how much money he really has. These are not trivial matters. But are they the most important? How many people are living the life of Christ in grace, and how fervently? How many people are making a sincere effort to improve their life of faith in spite of the burdens and temptations presented by our secular culture? How many people pray? How often? How well? What sacrifices are people making in order to remain faithful to the teaching of the Lord and his church?

The real state of the church is not something that we can weigh or perceive or judge. Only God really knows how his kingdom is doing at any given moment.

Moreover, the questions we all ask about the state of the church, natural as they are, may not even be appropriate. Perhaps it's not up to us to evaluate the church or gauge its level of success. Judgment belongs to the Lord, not to us. It's his church, not ours. If there were plenty of priests, if every Catholic in every parish came to mass every Sunday, if everybody knew all the catechism answers by heart, if parishioners contributed so generously that no parish had financial problems, would we then be justified in saying that the church was everything that Christ wants it to be? Surely not. It might be a church that was more complacent, a church that could take greater satisfaction in its achievements, but it would not necessarily be the church that Christ has in mind for us.

Our deficiencies and weaknesses are obvious and the

areas that need improvement are clear. Moreover, the forces ranged against us are mighty. Yet at the heart of it all is the mystery of God's love for us. This is why Jesus said, "Do not be afraid, little flock, for it has pleased your Father to give you the kingdom." (Luke 12, 32) This suggests to me that Christ wants us to take joy in being part of his people. He calls us and makes us his own. We are all invited to enjoy his company now and in the age to come. Christ invites us to keep trying, in every way we can, to come still closer to him, to bring others into deeper intimacy with him. None of us, no group of us, can ever say that we have accepted all the gifts that Christ offers us, simply because Christ is always offering us more. That's why there is always more to receive in the church and in the parish, always more to do. Yet our task is not to despair at the magnitude of the task, but to respond in joyful gratitude to God's love for us that is manifested in Christ, a love so great that no answer we make to it is ever complete.

The church has always been in a mess in one way or another. Yet the church has always been flourishing because it is the sign of God's love for his people. Our calling is to try to welcome that love ever more fully into ourselves and into our world. That's all.

Mother Teresa of Calcutta says that God does not call us to success, but to faithfulness.

Questions for Reflection

1. In what ways do you think the church of today is worse off than it was before?

2. In what ways do you think it is better?

3. What is really important in the life of the church?

WHERE ARE WE GOING?

It's hard to evaluate how well the church and its parishes are doing at a given moment because we aren't sure what questions we should ask to arrive at such an evaluation and, even if we were, only God would have all the necessary data to make a final judgment.

For those same reasons, it is difficult to guess how things will go in the future. Does God have some surprises in store for us, surprises like the Second Vatican Council which has affected the church in a way that nobody expected before the council began? What will be the long-term effect of an increasingly well-educated and prosperous Catholic laity? How will the smaller numbers of priests affect the church in our country in the long run? Will the secularism of our society continue to grow to the point that religious values are seen as totally irrelevant to "real life," or will our social evils call us back to an awareness that no society can survive unless its people share an awareness of real right and wrong? None of us can really answer questions like these.

Yet it may be that we can guess about the future by looking at the challenges and opportunities that we face now. The way in which we respond to these will surely have its effect on the decades ahead. Obviously any such analysis is necessarily a personal one, because different people will come up with a different list of challenges, and therefore a different focus on the future. I personally believe that there are three areas of particular present interest for Christian believers, three contexts that will have a strong effect on the future of parish and church in our country.

The first is education. We Catholics have to realize that we are living in an increasingly hostile atmosphere. The values that used to be taken for granted by everybody are now either rejected or neglected. Among these values are the sanctity of human life, the permanence of marriage, the nobility of self-sacrifice, the necessity of patience in adversity and pain and, perhaps most important of all, an acceptance that we are not the arbiters of our own destiny but rather dependent on Someone beyond ourselves for our ultimate fulfillment. While our culture may still pay lip service to ideals such as these, in practice it does not esteem them highly. As Catholic Christian believers, we do.

This means that we have to be stronger in our beliefs than we were before, simply because we receive so little support in them from the world around us. In order to have the kind of strength we require to face up to that world, we need to be quite clear about what Christ and his church teach—and why.

We need to grasp the implications of God's creative love for us, of sin and our need for redemption, of the destiny that is ours as individuals and as human community. Without basics like these, we run the risk of reducing our Catholic Christian faith to a set of cultural attitudes that make us feel good at Christmas and Easter, but are without much significance the rest of the time.

We have to know that there is a hard kernel of belief that is simply not up for grabs, that we are not free to fashion for ourselves a comfortable personal creed and moral code, but rather that we are held responsible for the way in which we respond to the truth of Christ and his church.

We also have to accept the fact that our faith makes demands on us, sometimes costly demands. Things that other people find tolerable or even virtuous are really not so, and we have to be prepared to face up to being different, to marching to a different drummer.

I believe that, for the short term at least, our Catholic Christian faith will be increasingly countercultural, increasingly out of step with the world around us. We have to respond to that reality, and one of the basic ways to make that response is through education.

We need to prepare our young people to live in a world which is at the same time attractive and alien. I am personally convinced that Catholic schools (and good religious education programs where the Catholic school is not realistically available) are crucially important to the future of Catholic faith in our country.

We need to educate adults in the implications of our faith for daily life. We need to help people understand the significance of what they see on TV, on the billboards, in the newspaper. For adults, the basic medium of education is probably the Sunday homily.

And this brings me to the second major challenge that I believe will affect the future of church and parish, and that challenge is the question of Sunday mass attendance.

In the last chapter I suggested that mere numbers are not necessarily a valid indication of the overall health of the church. But the fact remains that God's people need to worship together if they are to maintain their identity and that the Sunday liturgy is the prime occasion of the church's corporate worship. At the Sunday mass we hear God's word proclaimed and explained and we make our response with the gift of ourselves in prayer and holy communion. It is difficult, perhaps impossible, for people to stay aware of the meaning of their faith and to maintain that faith as the center of their lives if they do not refresh it with weekly shared eucharist.

Mass attendance is on the decline in our country, as I mentioned earlier. The most troubling aspect of that decline is that we can't really explain it. Personal opinions abound, but, as far as I am aware, there is no scientific research to account convincingly for this troubling phenomenon. Some say that the same percentage of Catholics are attending Sunday mass today as did in the past, but that they are going less regularly. That's some comfort, of course, but not much. I am inclined to think that finding a way to bring all Catholics to regular church attendance will be an important element of our future.

The third challenge that we face as we look toward the future is the challenge of the quality of priestly ministry. I do not mean to suggest in any way that the priestly ministry of today is deficient. Our priests work hard. They are dedicated to the Lord and the church and their people. The demands made on them have increased vastly over the past decades and they have responded generously to those demands. But something in me says that the demands and expectations will be different in the years that lie ahead of us.

I spoke earlier of the blessing of an increased participation in parish ministry by nonordained religious and lay people and I said that this gift offers priests the opportunity to concentrate more on specifically priestly tasks. I believe that the future will be significantly affected by the way in which our priests respond to the opportunity.

In the best scenario that I can imagine, the priest of the future will not need to deal with financial deficits or leaky roofs. He will not have to deal with every detail of the parish's ministry or attend every meeting. He will be the man of prayer and reflection, conspicuous for his personal knowledge of the Lord, able to speak in his preaching about the love of Christ in ways which address the very heart of his people. He will have time to reach out to those who are drifting away and to those who have never known Christ. He will be expected to be the leader of the parish, to be sure, but he will exercise that leadership role in a context of spiritual expertise that many parishioners do not look for from their priest today.

To bring that scenario to reality will require some change of expectations on the part of the parishioners and, perhaps, some change of priorities on the part of the priest. Extended times of prayer will be a part of his daily routine. He will begin to think about what he is to say to his people on Sunday at the very beginning of the previous week. He will spend some time every day with God's word in scripture and in serious theological and spiritual reading. He will know how to say "no" to demands on his time which are unreasonable, not because he is lazy but because he has more important things to do.

I believe that many priests are working toward those priorities now, and I am convinced that continued attention to them will be a major contribution to the future we are discussing.

Sound Catholic education, participation in the church's worship, the holiness of the church's priests: these are the things, in my opinion, that will determine the future of the church and its parishes. Each of them involves contact with the Lord. Sound education presents the Lord's teaching; the church's worship is worship in and with Christ; the holiness of the church's priests makes the holiness of Christ, the head of the church, more accessible to its people.

All this is another way of saying that the future of the church lies with Christ and is in his hands. But the hands of Christ work through the members of his body, the church. In a way, it all depends on him. In a way it all depends on us.

Questions for Reflection

1. What facets of the church's life do I see as particularly important for the church's future?

2. In what way is the church's present, as manifested in my parish, a sign of encouragement for the future?

3. What do I have to offer to the future of the church?

THE PERFECT PARISH

We have looked at what a parish is and what it is for and at some of the elements and activities that form its life. We have looked at the present and the future of parish. Perhaps it would now be useful to try to describe a perfect parish.

If we were to ask a priest what the perfect parish looks like, he would probably smile and say that it's a small place in the country with no school and no money problems.

A canon law expert might cite canon 515 and tell us that when you have a certain community of the faithful stably established under the care of a parish priest you have a canonically perfect parish.

In our planning process in the Archdiocese of Cincinnati, we say that every parish should be financially self-sufficient and ministerially complete. According to these criteria, a perfect parish would be one which provides, out of its own local resources, all the ministerial services which its people require for a fruitful Catholic Christian life, both within the parish community and in the secular world beyond it.

This suggests, first of all, that the perfect parish must be of a certain size. You simply can't do everything that needs to be done if there are only a few dozen parishioners. Moreover, chances are that if there are too few parishioners, there won't be enough money to pay salaries and keep the buildings in repair, and the congregation will find itself dependent on outside financial assistance or exhaust itself in endless and frantic fund raising. While there is no magic number of families or "units" required for a perfect parish, a parish cannot be perfect if it is too small.

A perfect parish gives considerable attention to the quality of its liturgical celebration. Not every parish has to be able to match the splendor of a papal mass in St. Peter's basilica, but every parish does have to strive to make the best use of the resources it has—musicians, readers, the church building and its sanctuary—to insure that the worship offered to God there is a nourishing experience for its people and gives appropriate expression to their love for God. It goes without saying that a perfect parish at the very least pays appropriate attention to the cleanliness and neatness of the church building.

A perfect parish is one in which the education of the parishioners is a high priority. If there is a school, its principal and teachers are carefully selected, professionally trained men and women who are aware of the purposes of Catholic schooling and who are eager to participate in the church's teaching mission. They know that the Catholic school has to have a different tone and different goals from public schools.

But even if there is no school, the perfect parish still engages in education. There is a good program of catechetics for all the young people of the parish, with clear goals and objectives at every level, and with good textbooks and teaching materials. The catechetical program is staffed by certified catechists who are aware of their responsibilities as agents of the church. The catechetical program has a share of the parish budget that is proportionate to its importance to the life of the parish. There are other educational programs, too: perhaps a lenten series of lectures in collaboration with other parishes, or a group that engages in reflection on the Bible. No adult member of the parish has to stop growing in knowledge and commitment due to the lack of local opportunities. As part of its educational mission, the perfect parish also encourages its members to engage in some regular Catholic reading. Many parishes help their members in this regard by subscribing to the diocesan newspaper for them.

The perfect parish is well organized. There are lots of opportunities for people to offer their talents in service to the local community on the parish council and on various parish commissions and committees, as members of bereavement ministries that help families with funeral arrangements and continue to comfort them in the weeks that follow, as visitors of the sick in the parish, as helpers in the catechetical program or the school. Parishes have found that people are also grateful when less pretentious opportunities for service are offered to them: responsibility for some of the gardening chores or a chance to spend a few hours a week helping with the physical maintenance of the buildings.

More than anything else, though, a perfect parish is a local Christian community in which people consciously reach out in love for one another. Good liturgy, attractive education programs, a high level of organization really don't mean much if the parishioners look on the parish as a kind of supermarket to which they go to get what they want but which calls for no investment of personal commitment from them. In the perfect parish you will find people standing around talking to one another before and after mass. They are on the lookout for new parishioners, to welcome them and make them feel at home. They are honestly interested in one another because they know that they are engaged together in a love affair with Christ and his church. They are women and men who assist the poor, the troubled, the dispossessed, and strive to create a more just society in the world outside the parish.

All this is not to say, however, that in the perfect parish everybody is a model of sanctity. There are those who are irregular in their attendance. There are those who drop out for a brief or even a long period of time. There are members who are on the outs with one another. And there is the regular celebration of the sacrament of reconciliation to demonstrate that sin is still present in the lives of the parishioners. A perfect parish is not composed exclusively of perfect people, but is rather a cross-section of good and bad, fervent and indifferent, a mixed bag of all the shades and tones of humanity just like the church universal. A parish which tried to exclude the imperfect would be a profoundly imperfect parish because it would not be reflecting the Jesus who came to save the wounded and the lost.

Nor does everything always go smoothly in a perfect parish. There may be honest differences of opinion about how things should be done and what level of priority should be given to the different elements of the parish's life.

Sometimes a parish will enter on a time of more than ordinary stress if, for example, the pastor doesn't seem to get along well with the people or if the parish council doesn't seem to be representing the parish at large. Building programs and fund drives, renovation of the sanctuary, a change of the school principal or in school policy about uniforms, new textbooks in the catechetical program—any one of these matters can plunge a parish into struggles that seem utterly foreign to its nature as a loving Christian community. Often struggles like these evoke depths of unkindness and rancor that surprise even those who are guilty of them. These struggles don't necessarily mean that the parish is falling apart, though. They are simply signs that the parish is composed of imperfect human beings who still have some growing to do. These periods of special stress need to be faced and dealt with kindly and patiently, because they are not without the potential for permanent harm. Their causes have to be identified and remedied. But the ability to deal with conflict in a Christlike fashion is itself one of the characteristics of the perfect parish.

The word "perfect" really means two different things. It means that which is without defect ("Here is a perfect rose.") but it also means that which has everything it is supposed to have in order to be what it is supposed to be ("A perfect square has four equal sides and four right angles.") We speak of perfect parishes in the second sense. A perfect parish is not one where there are no ragged edges, no unresolved problems, no areas that need improvement. A perfect parish is, rather, one in which priest and people are involved together, with the assistance of all the means that Christ and the church have put at their disposal, in the enterprise of being and becoming ever more deeply God's holy people.

A perfect parish, then, is not an ideal that exists in the mind of some theologian or an unattainable goal that we always pursue in vain. There are lots of perfect parishes around. It would not be surprising if many Catholics found themselves living in one now.

Questions for Reflection

1. How perfect is my parish?

2. How perfect a member am I?